D0296392

RECORD BUSTERS
MACHINES

CLIVE GIFFORD

WAYLAND

Published in 2014 by Wayland

Copyright © Wayland 2014

Wayland
338 Euston Road
London NW1 3BH

Wayland Australia
Level 17/207 Kent Street
Sydney NSW 2000

Editor: Nicola Edwards
Designer: Basement 68

A catalogue record for this book is available from the British Library.

ISBN: 978 0 7502 8110 2

Printed in China

Wayland is a division of Hachette Children's Books, an Hachette UK company.

www.hachette.co.uk

Abbreviations used:

m = metres
km = kilometres
cm = centimetres
mm = millimetres
kg = kilogrammes
g = grammes
km/h = kilometres per hour
°C = degrees Centigrade

Tricky words are listed in 'But What Does That Mean?' on page 31.

WHAT'S INSIDE?

AIRBUS A380-800 4

IROBOT ROOMBA 6

TMSUK T-52 ENRYU 7

ECOTRICITY *GREENBIRD* 8

BAGGER 293 10

INTERNATIONAL SPACE STATION 12

F1 POWERBOAT 14

MIL MI-26 16

KINGDA KA 18

MS *ALLURE OF THE SEAS* 20

SHOCKWAVE 22

NASA CRAWLER TRANSPORTER 23

ANTONOV AN-225 24

TIANHE-2 26

MICHIGAN MICRO MOTE 27

VOYAGER 1 28

TEST YOURSELF! 30

BUT WHAT DOES THAT MEAN? 31

CHECK IT OUT & INDEX 32

AIRBUS A380-800

The Airbus A380-800 is so big that some airports have had to change their facilities just to handle it. It has two passenger decks instead of one and, at a record-busting maximum, can carry up to 853 passengers.

BIGGEST AIRLINER!

An Airbus A380-800 on the ground at an air show. The airliner is 72.72m long and can fly up to 15,700km without refuelling.

WOW!

A BILLIONAIRE PRINCE HAS ORDERED HIS VERY OWN CUSTOMISED A380, COMPLETE WITH STEAM ROOM, HOT TUB, GRAND PIANO AND A GARAGE FOR HIS ROLLS ROYCE CAR!

Can you believe it?

The A380-800's four jet engines power the airliner to a top cruising speed of 945 km/h. The plane can weigh as much as 560,000kg when it takes off.

On the other hand...

The Bede BD-5 is the world's smallest and lightest jet aircraft, holding one person – the pilot – and weighing just 167kg.

The A380's wings measure 79.75m from one wingtip to the other. That's wider than a football pitch!

IROBOT ROOMBA

The world's biggest-selling robot is a disc-shaped vacuum cleaner. Since its invention in 2002, over six million Roomba robots have been sold.

MOST POPULAR ROBOT!

Can you believe it?

These 34cm-wide, 9cm-high robot vacuum cleaners find their way around a house all by themselves. If they come across an obstacle in their path, they steer round it.

The low-lying robot can even clean underneath pieces of furniture.

WOW!

SENSORS IN ITS BODY CAN SPOT A DROP AHEAD OF THE ROBOT SO THAT IT DOESN'T FALL DOWN STAIRS!

TMSUK T-52 ENRYU

Much, much bigger than a Roomba, the T-52 stands 3.45m high and 2.4m wide. Its two massive robot arms can each lift up to 500kg. That's the weight of 5 or 6 adults.

Can you believe it?

When fitted with a powerful gripper, the robot can rip off a car door to help rescuers reach people trapped inside.

The mighty T-52 lifts the weight of a car with ease.

WOW!

THE T-52 CAN CUT AWAY METAL AND REMOVE WRECKAGE AT A DISASTER SCENE SO PEOPLE CAN BE RESCUED.

ECOTRICITY GREENBIRD

The *Greenbird* is a land yacht that whizzes along smooth sandy beaches or salt flats on small wheels. It had no engine and only uses wind to power its solid sail made of carbon fibre. In 2009, it raced to a world record speed of 203.1km/h.

Greenbird makes its record-breaking run across Lake Ivanpah in California.

Can you believe it?

The *Greenbird* team have swapped its wheels for skis as they plan to become the fastest wind-powered vehicle on ice.

WOW!

THANKS TO GREENBIRD'S CLEVER DESIGN IT CAN TRAVEL 3-5 TIMES FASTER THAN THE SPEED OF THE WIND THAT IS BLOWING AROUND IT.

CONTENDERS

The Winston Wong Bio-Inspired Ice Vehicle (below) has an engine which powers a propeller blade at its rear. This pushes the vehicle on its skis to speeds of up to 130km/h. It has been used to race across snow and ice in Antarctica.

BAGGER 293

The Bagger 293 is an enormous digger used for mining coal on the land's surface. At 225m long, it is longer than two football pitches!

Can you believe it?

The Bagger 293 is 91m tall and weighs around 14,000 tonnes. It has 18 steel buckets which dig into the ground as the giant wheel turns. These buckets tip the earth and coal onto a long conveyor belt.

No rest for the Bagger 293 or the five workers controlling it as it works through the night in a mine in Germany.

10

The Bucyrus RH400 shovel is a digger with a single bucket. This bucket can hold over 90 tonnes of earth and rock. The driver's cab even has a kitchen with a fridge and microwave so the driver can eat lunch in the vehicle!

A workman (below) is dwarfed by the giant steel arm of the Bagger 293 as its buckets dig away the earth to recover coal.

WOW!

EACH DAY, THE BAGGER 293 DIGS UP ENOUGH EARTH TO FILL 96 OLYMPIC-SIZED SWIMMING POOLS!

11

INTERNATIONAL SPACE STATION

LARGEST SPACE MACHINE!

The International Space Station (ISS) is 109m long, longer than a football pitch, and has as much space to work and live in as a five-bedroomed house. The major difference is that it's been flying high above Earth since 2000.

Can you believe it?

It's taken over 100 spaceflights to build the ISS piece by piece from its many laboratory and living modules to its giant solar panels which provide the space station with power. Overall, the ISS cost around £75,000 million to build!

A spacewalk outside the ISS. A crew of up to seven astronauts live and work on the station for months at a time.

WOW!

THE ISS WEIGHS OVER 420,000KG – MORE THAN 320 MOTOR CARS! ITS SPEED AS IT ORBITS EARTH IS 27,743KM/H – THAT'S 7.7KM EVERY SECOND!

On the other hand...

The cabin of the tiny Mercury space capsule was just 1.9m wide and 2m tall – just enough room for a single astronaut to be crammed inside.

The ISS flies over 330km above Earth's surface and orbits the planet 15-16 times each day.

F1 POWERBOAT

F1 Powerboats are the fastest speedboats around. They are raced around water courses at lightning speeds of up to 240km/h.

A six-metre-long powerboat skims across the ocean surface. The orange wing mirrors allow the pilot to see who's behind!

Can you believe it?

An F1 Powerboat weighs about 500kg. It can accelerate from standing still to over 90km/h in just two seconds and can reach 160km/h in only four seconds. That's fast!

UP CLOSE

Pilots sit inside a strong box inside the boat called a safety cell when they race. The powerboats have no brakes and the racers control the speed by pressing a pedal with their foot.

WOW!

THE FASTEST EVER POWERBOAT WAS THE *SPIRIT OF AUSTRALIA* BUILT BY WATER-SPEED RECORD-HOLDER KEN WARBY. IT RACED TO A RECORD-BUSTING SPEED OF 511KM/H!

MIL MI-26

Built in Russia, the Mil Mi-26 is the world's largest helicopter. Its body is 35.9m long and it's lifted up into the air by eight giant rotor blades which are each 16m long.

An Mi-26 can travel up to 800km per flight with a top speed of 255km/h.

Can you believe it?

Most helicopters can hold just a few passengers. The Mil Mi-26 can hold up to 90, plus a crew of five. It can also transport huge machines such as tanks or giant bulldozers.

On the ground in Tver, Russia, the Mi-26 is one big beast, standing over 6m wide and 8.1m high.

МИ·26Т

WOW!

IN 1999, A MI-26 CARRIED A 24-TONNE BLOCK OF ICE ACROSS RUSSIA. THE GIANT ICE CUBE CONTAINED A FROZEN WOOLLY MAMMOTH THAT WAS 23,000 YEARS OLD!

VERTICAL-T

On the other hand...

The 6.5cm long Nano-Falcon (above) is one of the smallest remote-controlled helicopters ever. It weighs only 11 grams and is powered by a tiny electric motor normally used to make a mobile phone vibrate.

KINGDA KA

Dare you ride the 139m-high Kingda Ka rollercoaster in the United States? At the top of its giant hill, the train suddenly swoops down a vertical drop of 127m – that's like falling from the top of a 45-floor building!

Can you believe it?

Made of steel, Kingda Ka opened in 2005 and handles 1,400 brave passengers per hour. Riders reach speeds of 206km/h on the fastest part of its 950m-long track.

Whooah! Thrillseekers ride to the top of Kinga Ka's top hat tower, 139m above the ground.

18

CONTENDERS

At speeds of 240km/h, only one rollercoaster so far is faster than Kingda Ka: Formula Rosso in Abu Dhabi. One of the longest rollercoasters is Japan's Steel Dragon. It hurtles along on a 2,479m track.

Whooooooahhh! Riders thunder down a spiralling bend before Kingda Ka's magnetic brakes bring it safely to a stop.

WOW!

KINGDA KA'S POWERFUL LAUNCHER FIRES THE TRAIN ALONG THE TRACK SO THAT IT REACHES OVER 200KM/H IN JUST 3.5 SECONDS.

19

MS ALLURE OF THE SEAS

BIGGEST PASSENGER SHIP!

All aboard the 362m-long giant cruise liner – it's more like a floating town than a ship! The MS *Allure of the Seas* can carry up to 6,318 passengers on its 16 passenger decks, as well as more than 2,000 crew members.

The MS Allure of the Seas towers 65m above the ocean surface. The ship is 66m wide and weighs over 225,000 tonnes.

Can you believe it?

Among the ship's amazing features are two climbing walls, an ice skating rink, a basketball court (left) and a giant theatre. There's even a wave pool for surfing!

WOW!

THE MS *ALLURE OF THE SEAS* IS WIDER THAN THE WINGSPAN OF A BOEING 747 JUMBO JET. IT EVEN FEATURES A PARK WITH 12,000 PLANTS.

CONTENDERS

The longest ship of all was the Knock Nevis (also called the Seawise Giant) supertanker. At 458.45m long, this was a monster oil tanker!

RoyalCaribbean
INTERNATIONAL

SHOCKWAVE

Large trucks are sometimes called rigs. Shockwave is a big rig with a difference... it's fitted with three jet plane engines! These power it to a top speed of 605km/h, making it the fastest truck in the world.

A popular sight at car and truck festivals and airshows, Shockwave races along a runway with flames blazing out from the back of its jet engines.

Can you believe it?

Shockwave uses a huge amount of fuel – over 900 litres for every kilometre it races. Some of this is injected into the back of the jet engines to create eye-catching 10m-long flames to thrill spectators.

NASA CRAWLER TRANSPORTER

NASA's giant crawler transporters move heavy spacecraft, such as the Space Shuttle, around on the ground. These crawlers have a top speed when fully loaded of just 1.6km/h!

Can you believe it?

A Shuttle crawler weighs 2.7 million kg and has tanks that can hold 19,000 litres of diesel fuel. The crawler uses 297 litres of fuel for every one kilometre it travels.

WOW!

THE CRAWLER RUNS ON METAL TREADS LIKE A TANK BUT MUCH LARGER. EACH LINK IN THE TREAD IS 2.28M LONG AND WEIGHS 900KG, AND THERE ARE MORE THAN 450 OF THEM!

The crawler carries a fully loaded shuttle and fuel tanks weighing 2 million kg.

ANTONOV AN-225

Built in Russia, the Antonov An-225 is the world's biggest and heaviest aircraft. 84m long and measuring 88.4m from wingtip to wingtip, it needs six giant jet engines to lift it into the air.

LARGEST AIRCRAFT!

The An-225 soars through the air, reaching a top speed of 850km/h.

UR-82060

Can you believe it?

The An-225's cargo bay can be filled with large trucks, tanks and fire engines. Fully loaded, it can weigh up to 640,000kg. That's the weight of four Airbus A300 airliners.

On the other hand...

Micro aerial vehicles are remote controlled mini planes which can be used for spying. Some have a wingspan smaller than 10cm and weigh less than 300g.

WOW!

THE FIRST AIRCRAFT FLIGHT WAS MADE IN 1903 BY THE WRIGHT BROTHERS. THE TOTAL DISTANCE OF THAT FIRST FLIGHT WAS SHORTER THAN THE LENGTH OF THE CARGO BAY OF THE AN-225!

On the ground, the An-225 rests on 32 wheels, more than any other aircraft. Its nose cone hinges upwards for loading and unloading.

ANTONOV 225

INTERNATIONAL CARGO TRANSPORTER

TIANHE-2

Built in China, the Tianhe-2 is a massive supercomputer. It can perform thousands of billions of calculations every second and is used for really complicated maths!

The hugely powerful Tianhe-2 has more than 80,000 processor chips all working together to give extreme computing speed.

Can you believe it?

The Tianhe-2 is faster than 338 million regular personal computers all working together!

On the other hand...

The Hanwell Dekatron takes 10 seconds just to multiply two numbers together. Built in 1951, it is 6m wide and weighs 2,500kg but has less computer power than your mobile phone! It is the oldest computer still working today.

MICHIGAN MICRO MOTE

The Michigan Micro Mote, or M3 is a complete computer with a difference... it's tiny! The M3 measures just 1mm square but has a processor – the brain of a computer – memory and can communicate wirelessly with other computers.

◀ M3

Can you believe it?

The M3 is powered by tiny solar panels which need 90 minutes of sunlight or 10 hours of indoor light to power up. The minicomputer may soon be fitted to patients to check the health of their blood, eyes or heart.

WOW!

15 M3S CAN FIT ON A SINGLE COIN LIKE THE ONE ABOVE. IN CONTRAST THE EARLY AN/FSQ-7 COMPUTER COVERED 2,000 SQUARE METRES!

VOYAGER 1

FURTHEST MACHINE FROM EARTH!

Voyager 1, launched from Earth in 1977, is still travelling! Now more than 18,000 million km away from our planet, it is leaving the Solar System.

Voyager 1 passed close by the planets Jupiter and Saturn (above) on its long-distance journey.

Weighing 722kg with a 3.7m-wide radio dish, Voyager 1 has just 70 kilobytes of computer memory, a tiny fraction of the memory found in any mobile phone.

Can you believe it?

Covering 1.4 million km a day, Voyager 1 moves fast. In the 10 seconds or so it takes you to read this sentence, it travels 190km – further than from London to Calais in France.

UP CLOSE

Voyager 1 still sends and receives messages using its radio dish. Radio waves from the space probe take more than 16 hours to reach Earth.

WOW!

JUST IN CASE IT MEETS ANY ALIENS, VOYAGER 1 IS CARRYING A GOLD DISC (RIGHT) CONTAINING IMAGES OF EARTH AND GREETINGS IN 55 LANGUAGES.

TEST YOURSELF!

Can you remember facts about the record-busting machines in this book? Test yourself here by answering these questions!

1. Which machine is longer, a Bagger 293 or the MS Allure of the Seas?

2. From which country is the world's fastest computer?

3. Which machine transported a woolly mammoth frozen in a block of ice?

4. What was the name of the world's fastest speedboat?

5. How many Ms computers can fit on to a single coin?

6. How many jet engines power the Shockwave truck?

7. Do passengers on the Kingda Ka rollercoaster go from 0-200km/h in 3.5, 5.5 or 7.5 seconds?

8. Which devices give the International Space Station its power?

9. Which vehicle has travelled fastest: the Shuttle Crawler, the Winston Wong Bio-Inspired Ice Vehicle or the Greenbird?

10. How many jet engines does the Antonov An-225 have?

Answers
1. MS Allure of the Seas
2. China
3. The Mil Mi-26 helicopter
4. Spirit of Australia
5. Fifteen
6. Three
7. 3.5 seconds
8. Solar panels
9. Greenbird
10. Six

BUT WHAT DOES THAT MEAN?

cab The part of a truck or digger where the driver sits and controls the vehicle.

carbon fibre A material which is light in weight but very strong.

cargo bay The area in some aircraft and helicopters where objects to be transported are stored.

cruise liner A large passenger ship used for long pleasure trips.

cruising speed The speed at which a vehicle tends to run. This is slower than its maximum speed.

launcher A machine producing the power to start a rollercoaster ride.

living module The part of the ISS where the astronauts eat and sleep.

processor A computer chip that helps to control a computer or other machine.

robots Machines that can work by themselves and take in information about their surroundings.

rotor blade The long, thin blades spun by a helicopter's engine that act like wings and lift the craft into the air.

safety cell A strong box or cabin that protects the driver of a powerboat.

salt flats A large area of usually flat and smooth land left when saltwater has evaporated.

sensors Devices which give a robot information about itself or its surroundings.

solar panels Panels with solar cells which convert sunlight into electricity.

space probe An unmanned machine sent used to explore space.

treads Enormous belts or tracks like large versions of those on a tank which turn to move the Shuttle Crawler.

wingspan The measurement of the wings of an aircraft from one wingtip to the other.

wirelessly A way of sending signals between different machines without using wires or cables.

woolly mammoth A large prehistoric creature that looked like a big furry elephant and weighed around 6,000kg.

CHECK IT OUT & INDEX

Check out these amazing places to go and websites to visit!

The Helicopter Museum, Weston-super-Mare, England
Check out dozens of real helicopters here!

Diggerland, Kent, Devon, Durham, Yorkshire, England
Four theme parks, all packed with diggers!

Six Flags Great Adventure, New Jersey, USA
Home of the mighty Kingda Ka!

Kennedy Space Center, Florida, USA
See a real Space Shuttle and the world's most powerful rocket, the Saturn V.

http://kids.discovery.com/games/build-play/build-a-coaster
Create your own rollercoaster at this fun site.

http://www.guinnessworldrecords.com/Search.aspx?q=aircraft
Check out this collection of aircraft world records.

http://www.nasa.gov/mission_pages/station/main/index.html#.Ueec4I2866U
Find pictures and videos of the International Space Station here, as well as interviews and features on life in space.

Index

A
acceleration 15, 19
airliners 4, 5, 24

C
cars 4, 7
computers 26, 27
crawler transporter 23

D
diggers 10, 11

E
engines 5, 8, 9, 22

F
fuel 22, 23

H
helicopters 16, 17

I
ice 8, 9, 17
International Space Station 12, 13

L
land yacht 8

P
passengers 4, 16, 18, 20
pilots 5, 15

R
robots 6, 7
rollercoasters 18, 19

S
ships 20, 21
size 4, 5, 10, 12, 13, 16, 17, 18, 20, 21, 24, 25, 27
skis 8, 9
spacecraft 23, 28, 29
speed 5, 8, 9, 13, 14, 15, 18, 19, 22, 23, 26, 29
speedboats 14, 15
strength 7

T
trucks 22, 24

W
weight 5, 13, 15, 24
wheels 8, 9

RECORD BUSTERS
Contents of new titles in the series:

BUGS
978 0 7502 8109 6

Goliath bird eating spider
Australian termite
Froghopper
Monarch butterfly
Cicada
Woolly bear caterpillar
Mayfly
Southern giant darner
Illacme plenipes
Chan's megastick
Queen Alexandra's birdwing
Hercules beetle
Worker honey bee
Collembola (Spingtails)
Anopheles mosquito
Brazilian wandering spider
Desert locust
Test Yourself!
But What Does That Mean?
Check It Out & Index

MACHINES
978 0 7502 8110 2

The Airbus A380-800
Irobot Roomba
Tmsuk T-52 Enryu
Ecotricity Greenbird
Bagger 293
International Space Station
F1 powerboat
Mil Mi-26
Kingda ka
MS Allure of the Seas
Shockwave
NASA crawler transporter
Antonov An-225
Tianhe-2
Michigan micro mote
Voyager 1
Test Yourself!
But What Does That Mean?
Check It Out & Index

DINOSAURS
978 0 7502 8108 9

Ankylosaurus
Sauroposeidon
Struthiomimus
Tyrannosaurus Rex
Utahraptor
Quetzalcoatlus
Spinosaurus
Therizinosaurus
Ceratopsians
Argentinosaurus
Elasmosaurus
Troodon
Edmontosaurus
Test Yourself!
But What Does That Mean?
Check It Out & Index

WORLD CUP FOOTBALL
978 0 7502 8107 2

Uruguay
Japan and South Korea
The Maracana
World Cup strikers
Oleg Salenko
Javier Hernandez
Australia v American Samoa
José Batista
Luis Suarez
Penalty shootouts
Brazil
Pelé
World Cup keepers
The USA women's team
Birgit Prinz and Marta
Test Yourself!
But What Does That Mean?
Check It Out & Index

WAYLAND
www.waylandbooks.co.uk